W9-DEM-004

JUN   1992

cRAZy
Alphabet

Text copyright © 1990 by Lynn Cox
Illustrations copyright © 1990 by Rodney McRae
First American Edition 1992 published by
Orchard Books
First published in Australia by Angus & Robertson
Publishers

Orchard Books
387 Park Avenue South
New York, NY 10016

Manufactured in the United States of America
Printed by General Offset Company, Inc.
Bound by Horowitz/Rae

Book design by Susan Phillips

10 9 8 7 6 5 4 3 2 1

The text of this book is set in 15 point Utopia.

Library of Congress Cataloging-in-Publication Data
Cox. Lynn.
   Crazy alphabet / by Lynn Cox ; illustrated by
Rodney McRae.
        p.   cm.
   Summary: A cumulative alphabet starting with an
apple and ending with a Yowie who eats everything
and bursts, leaving zero.
   ISBN 0-531-05966-9. — ISBN 0-531-08566-X
(lib. bdg.)
   1. English language — Alphabet — Juvenile
literature.
[1. Alphabet.]   I. McRae, Rodney, ill.   II. Title.
PE1155.C59   1992   [E] — dc20   91-3734

CRAZY
Alphabet

by **Lynn Cox**

illustrated by **Rodney McRae**

Orchard Books
New York

Aa

A is for Apple.

Everyone knows that.

Bb

B is for Bird

that ate the apple.

Cc

C is for Cat

that caught the bird
that ate the apple.

Dd

D is for Dog

that chased the cat
that caught the bird
that ate the apple.

Ee

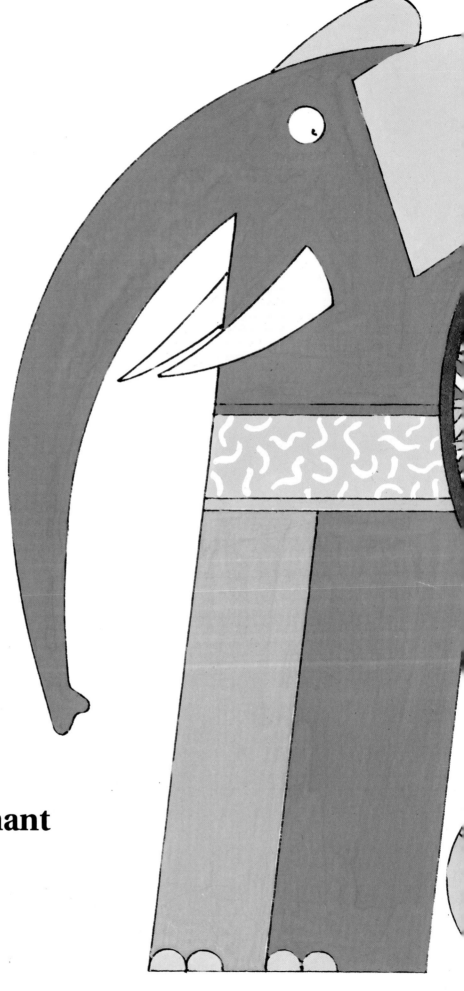

E is for Elephant

that sat on the dog
that chased the cat
that caught the bird
that ate the apple.

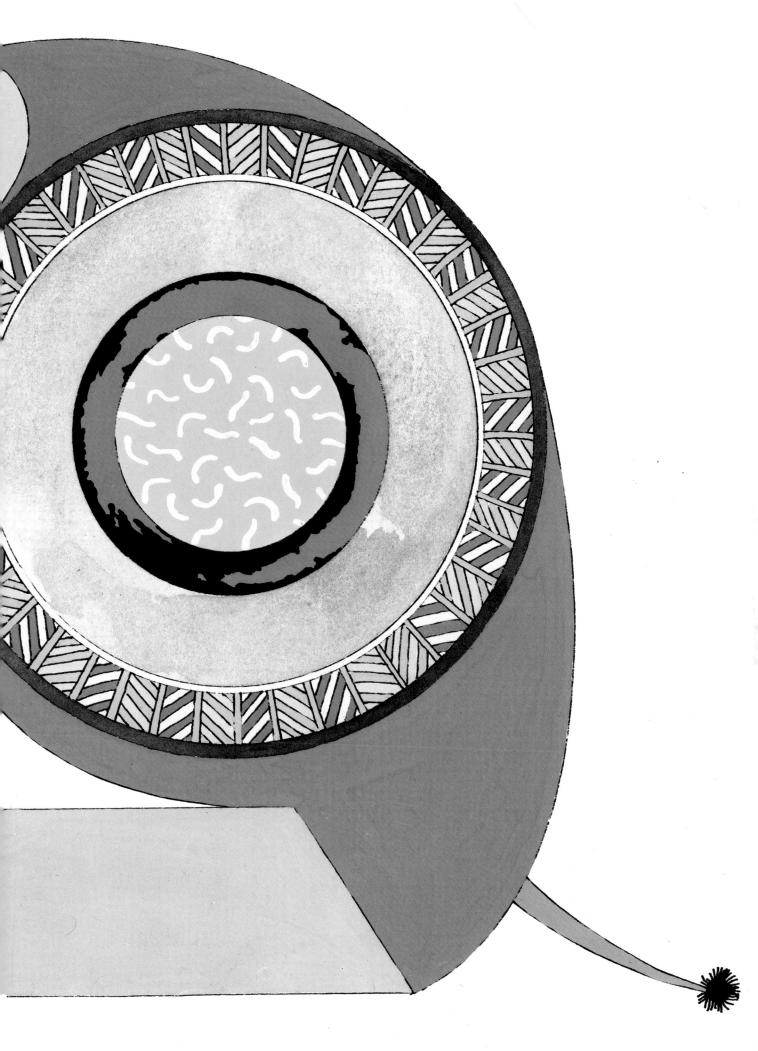

Ff

F is for Farmer

who scared the elephant
that sat on the dog
that chased the cat
that caught the bird
that ate the apple.

Gg

G is for Gun

the farmer used
to scare the elephant
that sat on the dog
that chased the cat
that caught the bird
that ate the apple.

Hh

H is for Hand

that held the gun
the farmer used
to scare the elephant
that sat on the dog
that chased the cat
that caught the bird
that ate the apple.

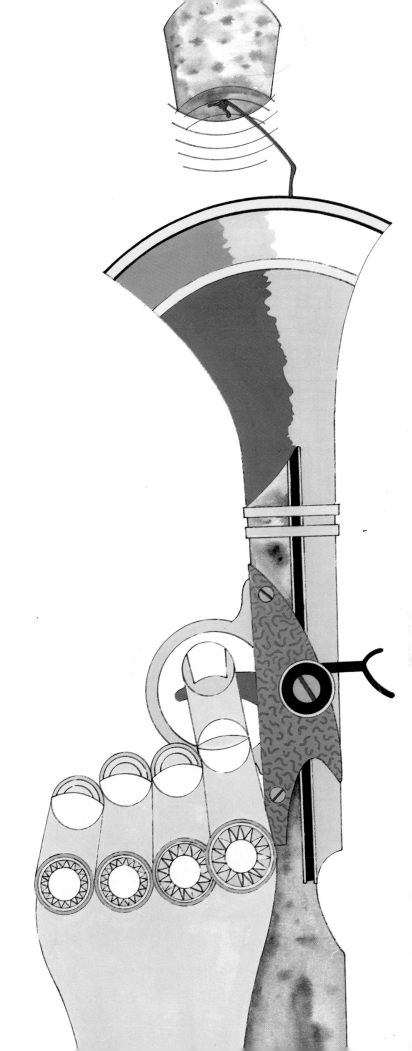

Ii

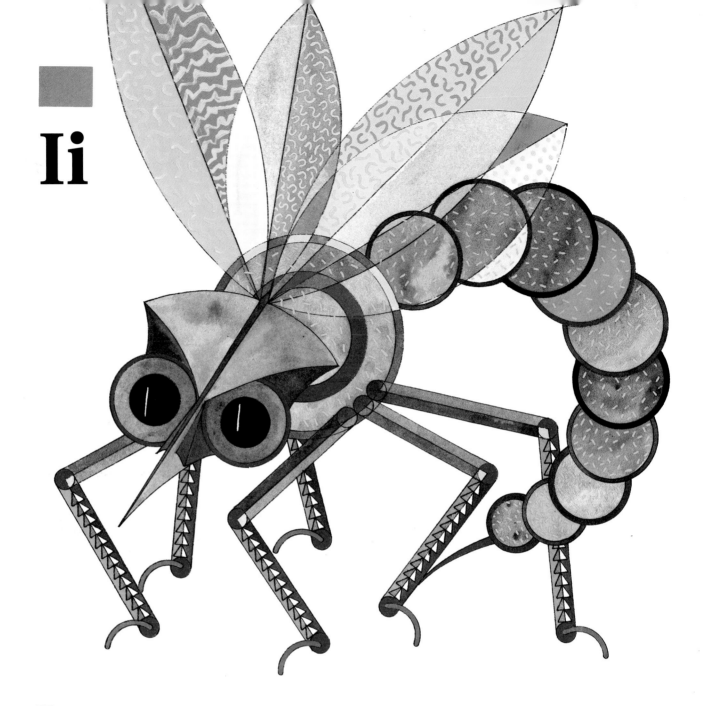

I is for Insect

that bit the hand
that held the gun
the farmer used
to scare the elephant
that sat on the dog
that chased the cat
that caught the bird
that ate the apple.

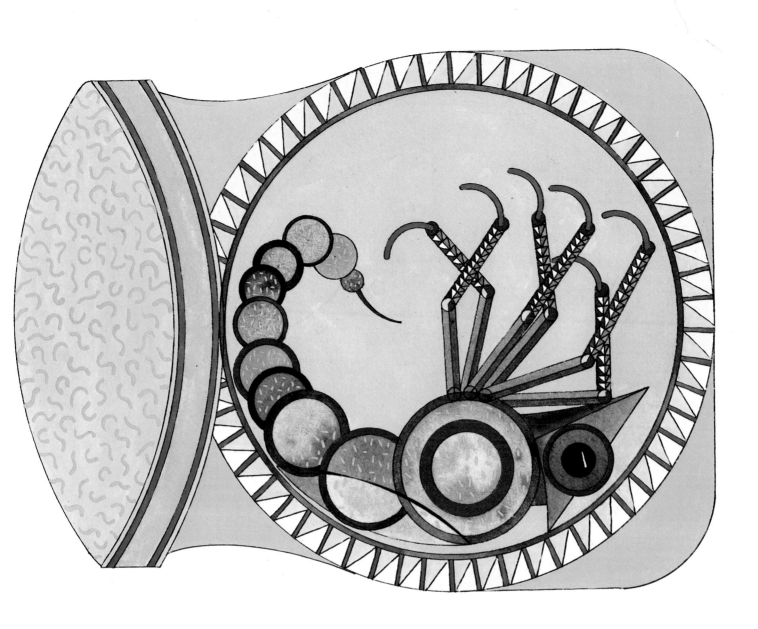

J is for Jar

Jj

that trapped the insect
that bit the hand
that held the gun
the farmer used
to scare the elephant
that sat on the dog
that chased the cat
that caught the bird
that ate the apple.

Kk

Ll

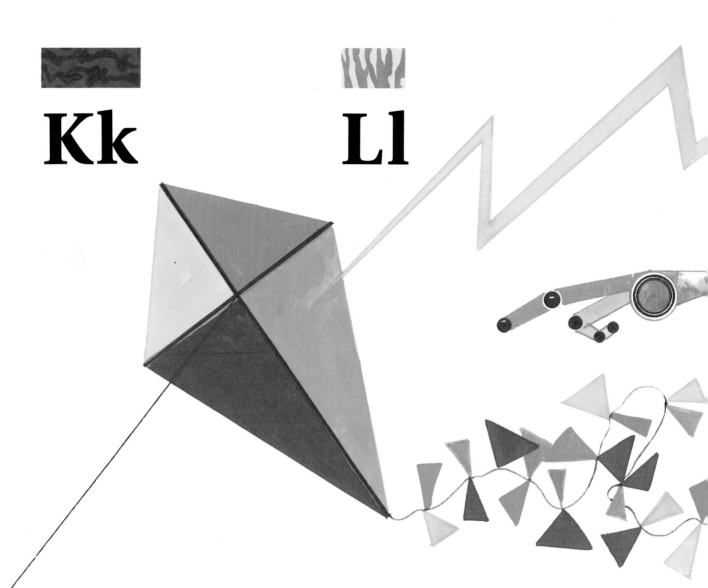

K is for Kite

tied to the jar
that trapped the insect
that bit the hand
that held the gun
the farmer used
to scare the elephant
that sat on the dog
that chased the cat
that caught the bird
that ate the apple.

L is for Lightning

that struck the kite
tied to the jar
that trapped the insect
that bit the hand
that held the gun
the farmer used
to scare the elephant
that sat on the dog
that chased the cat
that caught the bird
that ate the apple.

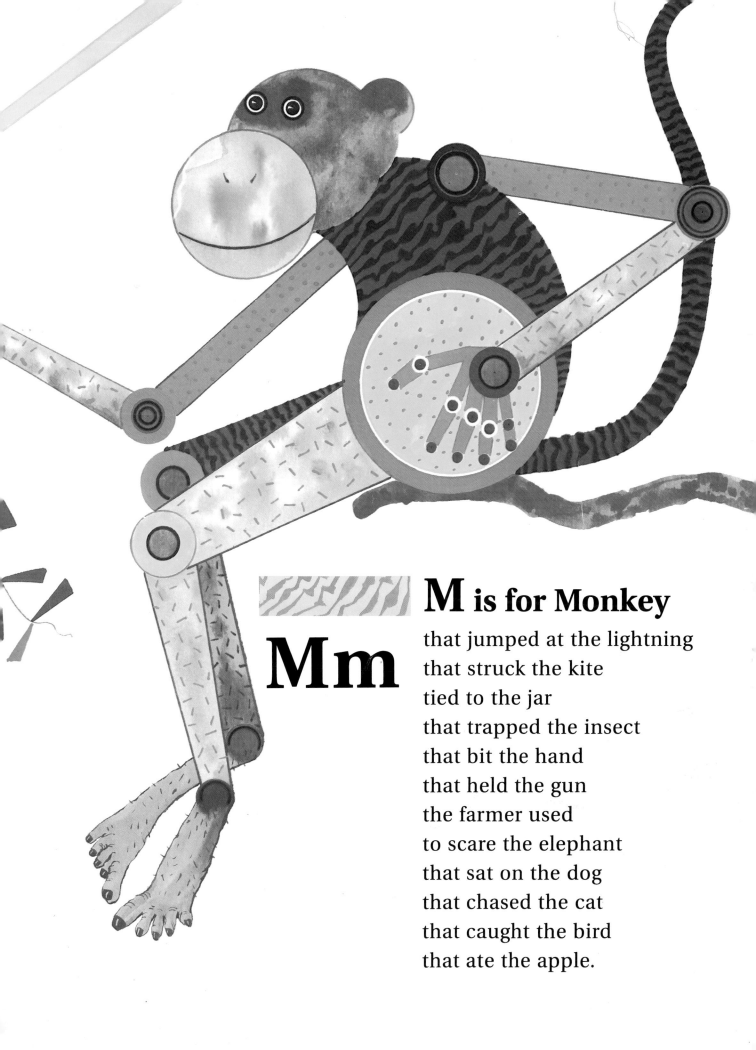

M is for Monkey

Mm

that jumped at the lightning
that struck the kite
tied to the jar
that trapped the insect
that bit the hand
that held the gun
the farmer used
to scare the elephant
that sat on the dog
that chased the cat
that caught the bird
that ate the apple.

Nn

N is for Nut

that hit the monkey
that jumped at the lightning
that struck the kite
tied to the jar
that trapped the insect
that bit the hand
that held the gun
the farmer used
to scare the elephant
that sat on the dog
that chased the cat
that caught the bird
that ate the apple.

Oo

O is for Oak

that dropped the nut
that hit the monkey
that jumped at the lightning
that struck the kite
tied to the jar
that trapped the insect
that bit the hand
that held the gun
the farmer used
to scare the elephant
that sat on the dog
that chased the cat
that caught the bird
that ate the apple.

Pp

P is for Parrot

perched in the oak
that dropped the nut
that hit the monkey
that jumped at the lightning
that struck the kite
tied to the jar
that trapped the insect
that bit the hand
that held the gun
the farmer used
to scare the elephant
that sat on the dog
that chased the cat
that caught the bird
that ate the apple.

Qq

Q is for Queen

who owned the parrot
perched in the oak
that dropped the nut
that hit the monkey
that jumped at the lightning
that struck the kite
tied to the jar
that trapped the insect
that bit the hand
that held the gun
the farmer used
to scare the elephant
that sat on the dog
that chased the cat
that caught the bird
that ate the apple.

Rr

R is for Robe

worn by the queen
who owned the parrot
perched in the oak
that dropped the nut
that hit the monkey
that jumped at the lightning
that struck the kite
tied to the jar
that trapped the insect
that bit the hand
that held the gun
the farmer used
to scare the elephant
that sat on the dog
that chased the cat
that caught the bird
that ate the apple.

Ss

S is for Soup

that spilled on the robe
worn by the queen
who owned the parrot
perched in the oak
that dropped the nut
that hit the monkey
that jumped at the lightning
that struck the kite
tied to the jar
that trapped the insect
that bit the hand
that held the gun
the farmer used
to scare the elephant
that sat on the dog
that chased the cat
that caught the bird
that ate the apple.

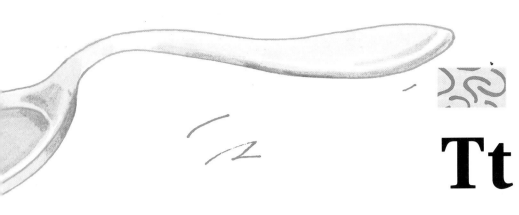

Tt

T is for Table

that held the soup
that spilled on the robe
worn by the queen
who owned the parrot
perched in the oak
that dropped the nut
that hit the monkey
that jumped at the lightning
that struck the kite
tied to the jar
that trapped the insect
that bit the hand
that held the gun
the farmer used
to scare the elephant
that sat on the dog
that chased the cat
that caught the bird
that ate the apple.

Uu

U is for Umbrella

that covered the table
that held the soup
that spilled on the robe
worn by the queen
who owned the parrot
perched in the oak
that dropped the nut
that hit the monkey
that jumped at the lightning
that struck the kite
tied to the jar
that trapped the insect
that bit the hand
that held the gun
the farmer used
to scare the elephant
that sat on the dog
that chased the cat
that caught the bird
that ate the apple.

Vv

V is for Vase

under the umbrella
that covered the table
that held the soup
that spilled on the robe
worn by the queen
who owned the parrot
perched in the oak
that dropped the nut
that hit the monkey
that jumped at the lightning
that struck the kite
tied to the jar
that trapped the insect
that bit the hand
that held the gun
the farmer used
to scare the elephant
that sat on the dog
that chased the cat
that caught the bird
that ate the apple.

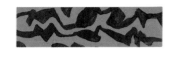

Ww

W is for Wombat

that buried the vase
from under the umbrella
that covered the table
that held the soup
that spilled on the robe
worn by the queen
who owned the parrot
perched in the oak
that dropped the nut
that hit the monkey
that jumped at the lightning
that struck the kite
tied to the jar
that trapped the insect
that bit the hand
that held the gun
the farmer used
to scare the elephant
that sat on the dog
that chased the cat
that caught the bird
that ate the apple.

Xx

X is for X

that marks the spot
the wombat used
to bury the vase
from under the umbrella
that covered the table
that held the soup
that spilled on the robe
worn by the queen
who owned the parrot
perched in the oak
that dropped the nut
that hit the monkey
that jumped at the lightning
that struck the kite
tied to the jar
that trapped the insect
that bit the hand
that held the gun
the farmer used
to scare the elephant
that sat on the dog
that chased the cat
that caught the bird
that ate the apple.

Yy

Y is for Yowie

that ate the X
and the wombat
and the vase
and the umbrella
and the table
and the soup
and the robe
and the queen
and the parrot
and the oak
and the nut
and the monkey
and the lightning
and the kite
and the jar
and the insect
and the hand
and the gun
and the farmer
and the elephant
and the dog
and the cat
and the bird
and the apple . . .

. . . and then burst!

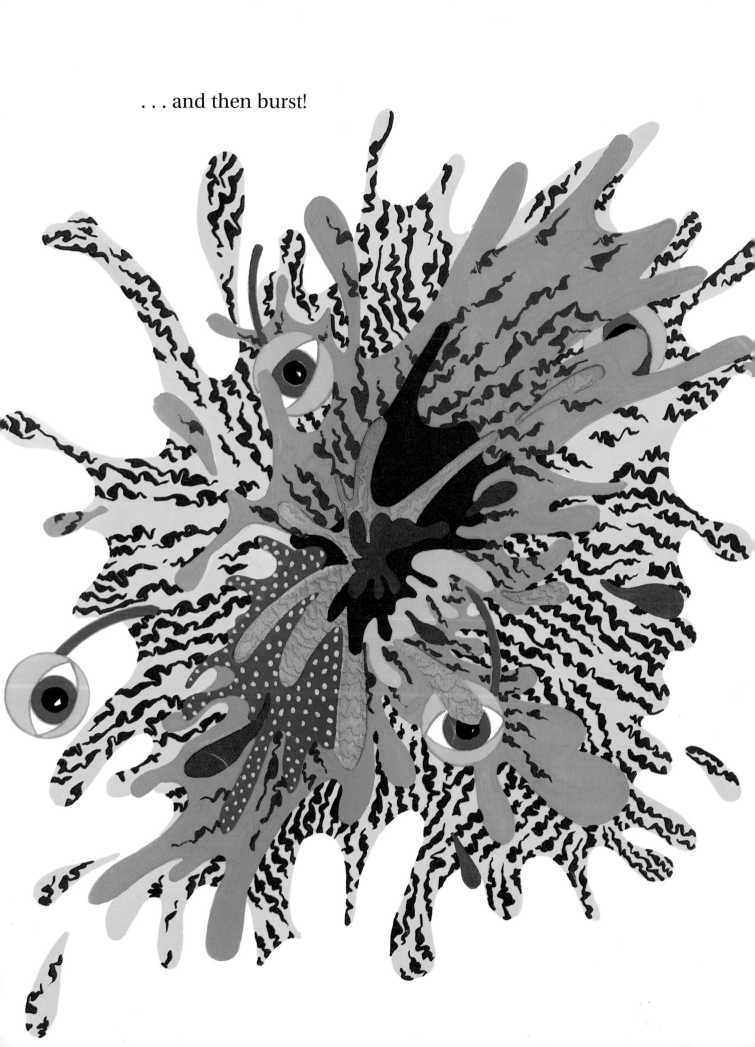

Zz

Z is for Zero,

all that is left
of the Yowie
that ate the X
and the wombat
and the vase
and the umbrella
and the table
and the soup
and the robe
and the queen
and the parrot
and the oak
and the nut
and the monkey
and the lightning
and the kite
and the jar
and the insect
and the hand
and the gun
and the farmer
and the elephant
and the dog
and the cat
and the bird
and the apple.

**See how much trouble you can start,
just by eating an apple?**